NORTH TYNESIDE LIBRARIES

3 8012 50200 1747

GW01164309

WITHDRAWN

Take-OFF!

Bug Books

MOSQUITO

Jill Bailey

Heinemann
LIBRARY

www.heinemann.co.uk
Visit our website to find out more information about Heinemann Library books.

To order:
- Phone 44 (0) 1865 888066
- Send a fax to 44 (0) 1865 314091
- Visit the Heinemann Bookshop at www.heinemann.co.uk to browse our catalogue and order online.

First published in Great Britain by Heinemann Library,
Halley Court, Jordan Hill, Oxford OX2 8EJ,
a division of Reed Educational and Professional Publishing Ltd.
Heinemann is a registered trademark of Reed Educational and Professional Publishing Ltd.

OXFORD   MELBOURNE   AUCKLAND
JOHANNESBURG   BLANTYRE   GABORONE
IBADAN   PORTSMOUTH (NH) USA   CHICAGO

© Reed Educational and Professional Publishing Ltd 2001

The moral right of the proprietor has been asserted.

All rights reserved. No part of this publication may be reproduced, stored in a retrieval system, or transmitted in any form or by any means, electronic, mechanical, photocopying, recording, or otherwise, without either the prior written permission of the publishers or a licence permitting restricted copying in the United Kingdom issued by the Copyright Licensing Agency Ltd, 90 Tottenham Court Road, London W1P 0LP.

Designed by Celia Floyd
Illustrated by Alan Male
Originated by Ambassador Litho ltd
Printed by South China Printing in Hong Kong/China

ISBN 0 431 01820 0 (hardback)   ISBN 0 431 01825 1 (paperback)
05 04 03 02 01   05 04 03 02 01
10 9 8 7 6 5 4 3 2 1   10 9 8 7 6 5 4 3 2 1

British Library Cataloguing in Publication Data

Bailey, Jill
    Mosquito. – (Bug books) (Take-off!)
    1.Mosquitoes – Juvenile literature
    I.Title
    595.7'72

Acknowledgements
The publishers would like to thank the following for permission to reproduce photographs:
Ardea London Ltd: R Gibbons p7, D Greenslade p4; Bruce Coleman Ltd: J Shaw p6, K Taylor p13; FLPA: D Grewcock p11, L West p21; Chris Honeywell p28; NHPA: G Bernard pp15, 17, 20, S Dalton pp26, 27, P Parks p9, J Shaw p23; Oxford Scientific Films: R Brown p22, J Cooke pp10, 14, 16, 18, 19; London Scientific Films: p12, H Taylor p29; Planet Earth Pictures: A Mounter p24; Science Photo Library: T Brain p5, A Crump p25, J Revy.

Cover photograph reproduced with permission of Bruce Coleman.

Our thanks to Sue Graves and Hilda Reed for their advice and expertise in the preparation of this book.

Every effort has been made to contact copyright holders of any material reproduced in this book. Any omissions will be rectified in subsequent printings if notice is given to the publishers.

Contents

What are mosquitoes?	4
Where do mosquitoes live?	6
What do mosquitoes look like?	8
What do mosquitoes do?	10
How long do mosquitoes live?	12
How are mosquitoes born?	14
How do mosquitoes grow?	16
How do baby mosquitoes change shape?	18
What do mosquitoes eat?	20
Which animals attack mosquitoes?	22
How are mosquitoes special?	24
How do mosquitoes move?	26
Thinking about mosquitoes	28
Bug map	30
Glossary	31
Index	32

Any words appearing in the text in bold, **like this**, are explained in the Glossary.

What are mosquitoes?

head
middle
abdomen

A mosquito's body has three sections.

Mosquitoes are insects. They have a body made up of three parts — a head, a middle and an **abdomen**. They have three pairs of legs and one pair of wings.

All insects have a body that has three sections. All insects have six legs, too.

4

eyes

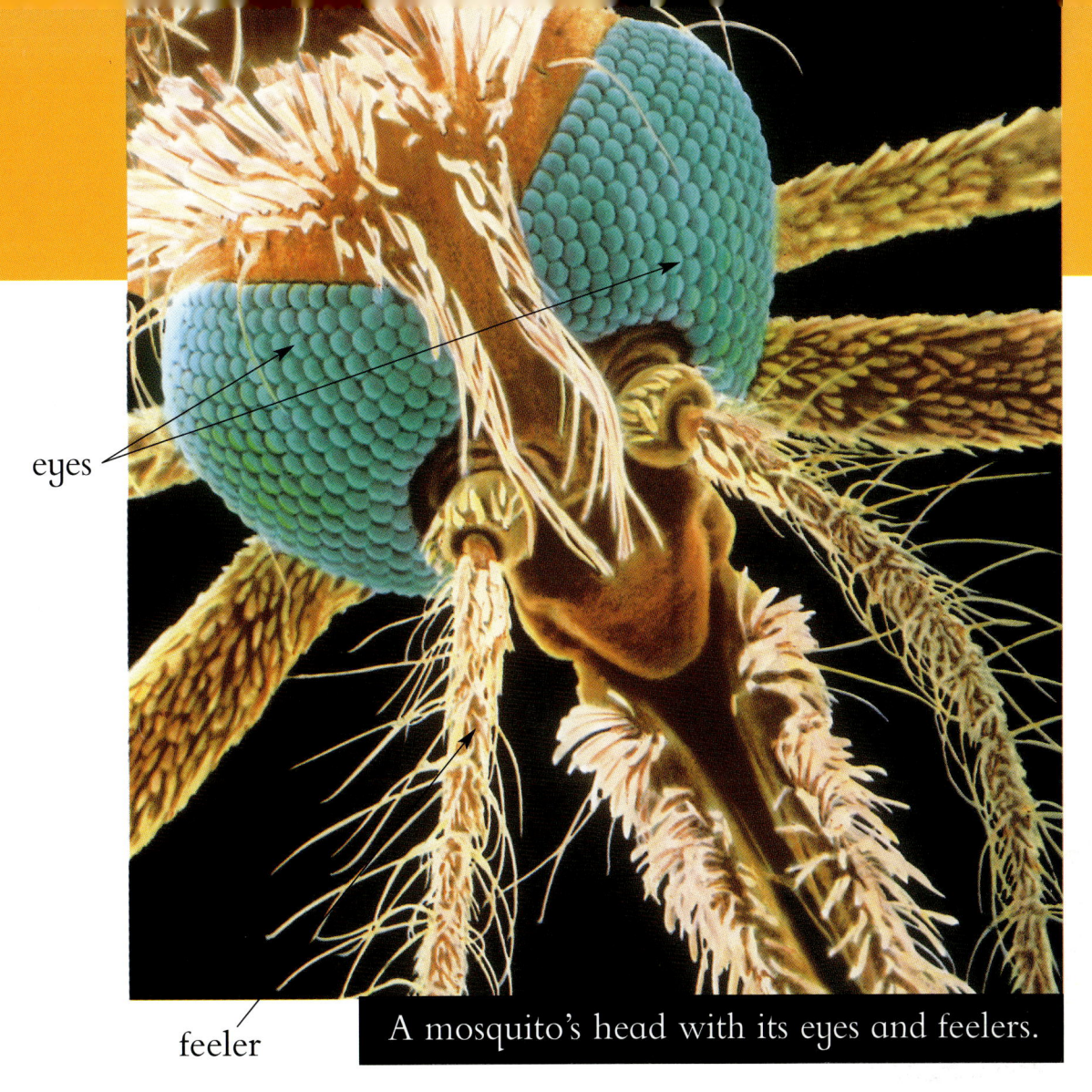

feeler A mosquito's head with its eyes and feelers.

A mosquito has huge eyes. On its head also are a pair of **feelers** for touching, smelling and hearing. Can you see the feelers and eyes on this mosquito?

Insects' eyes are made up of lots of cone-shaped parts.

5

Where do mosquitoes live?

Mosquitoes like to live in damp places like this.

pools of water

Mosquitoes live in damp shady places, near pools of water where their babies can live. Even small puddles are big enough for mosquito babies to live in.

Baby mosquitoes are like little wriggling grubs.

Mosquitoes often come into houses and rest on walls and ceilings. They live all over the world, especially in **tropical** forests and in the far north.

Mosquitoes can often be seen on walls in houses.

mosquito

What do mosquitoes look like?

Mosquitoes are small **insects**. The common house mosquito is about as long as a little fingernail. The males are thinner than the **females** and have beautiful feathery **feelers**.

feathery feeler

The common house mosquito is about 5–6 mm long. Measure 6 mm to find out how long a common house mosquito can be.

A male mosquito's feathery feelers.

Mosquitoes fly in a jerky up-and-down way, with their legs trailing below them. They rest with their wings folded.

mosquito

legs

There are more than 1600 different kinds of mosquito in the world.

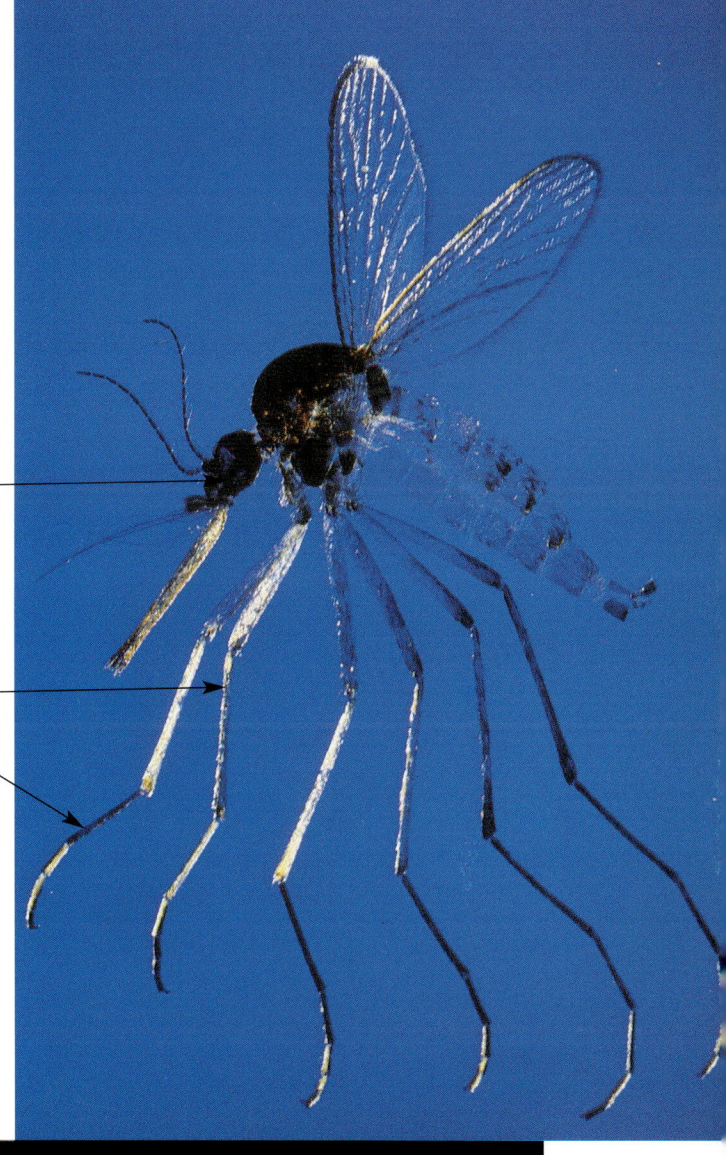

A flying mosquito with its trailing legs.

What do mosquitoes do?

A mosquito that has come out in the evening.

Many mosquitoes hide during the day. They come out in the evening when the air is cool and damp. They look for food and other mosquitoes.

swarm of mosquitoes

A **swarm** of thousands of mosquitoes.

Crowds of **male** mosquitoes 'dance' together to attract the **females**. The males' **feelers** listen for the whine of the females' wings. The male and female mosquitoes **mate**.

How long do mosquitoes live?

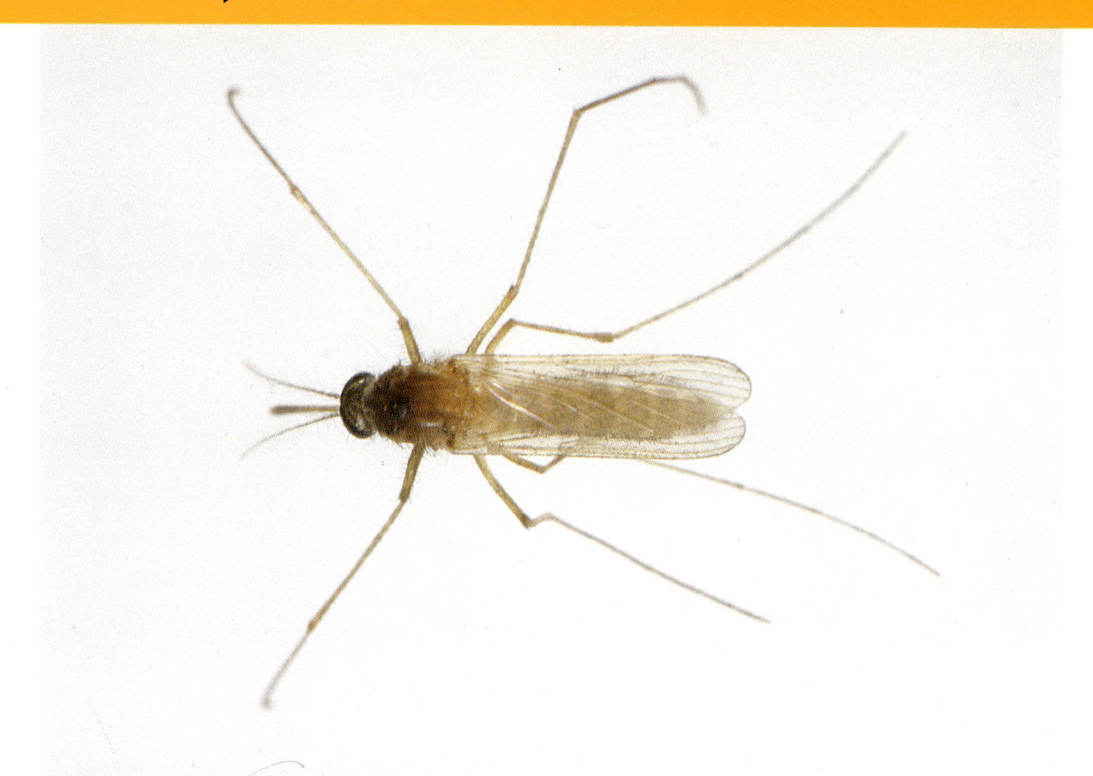

A female mosquito.

The **female** mosquitoes live longest, sometimes for 2–3 weeks. A few mosquitoes live much longer. They sleep through the winter in houses or **hollow** trees.

Mosquitoes lay their eggs in water in the spring and then die. In less than a month these eggs will **hatch**, become **pupae** and grow to be new **adult** mosquitoes ready to lay their own eggs.

A mosquito laying its eggs in water. Can you see its reflection?

How are mosquitoes born?

eggs

Mosquito eggs on the surface of the water.

water surface

The **female** house mosquito lays her eggs on the surface of a small pool or puddle. The eggs form a tiny **raft**.

A female house mosquito can lay up to 300 eggs at a time!

larvae

Tiny swimming larvae.

After a few hours, the eggs **hatch**. A tiny wriggling **larva** escapes through the bottom of each egg and swims off.

How do mosquitoes grow?

tube | Mosquito larvae breathing through their long tubes. | water surface

Baby mosquito **larvae** hang upside-down from the water surface. They breathe in air from a long tube. Can you see the long tubes on these larvae?

Baby mosquito larvae swim by wriggling.

hairs

The hairs around the larva's mouth sweeping water and food into its mouth.

Hairs surround the little larva's mouth. These hairs sweep water into the mouth. The larva eats tiny pieces of food floating in the water.

17

How do baby mosquitoes change shape?

The larva becoming a pupa.

pupa

When a **larva** gets big enough, it stops eating. Its head end gets very large and grows two little tubes to take in air. It is now called a **pupa**.

Inside its skin, the pupa slowly changes into an **adult** mosquito. The skin splits and the new mosquito climbs out and flies away.

mosquito

A mosquito splitting out of its pupa.

What do mosquitoes eat?

A male mosquito feeding on flower nectar.

flower

Male mosquitoes do not eat much. They suck up flower **nectar** through their long mouths. **Female** mosquitoes drink blood to help them make eggs.

female mosquito

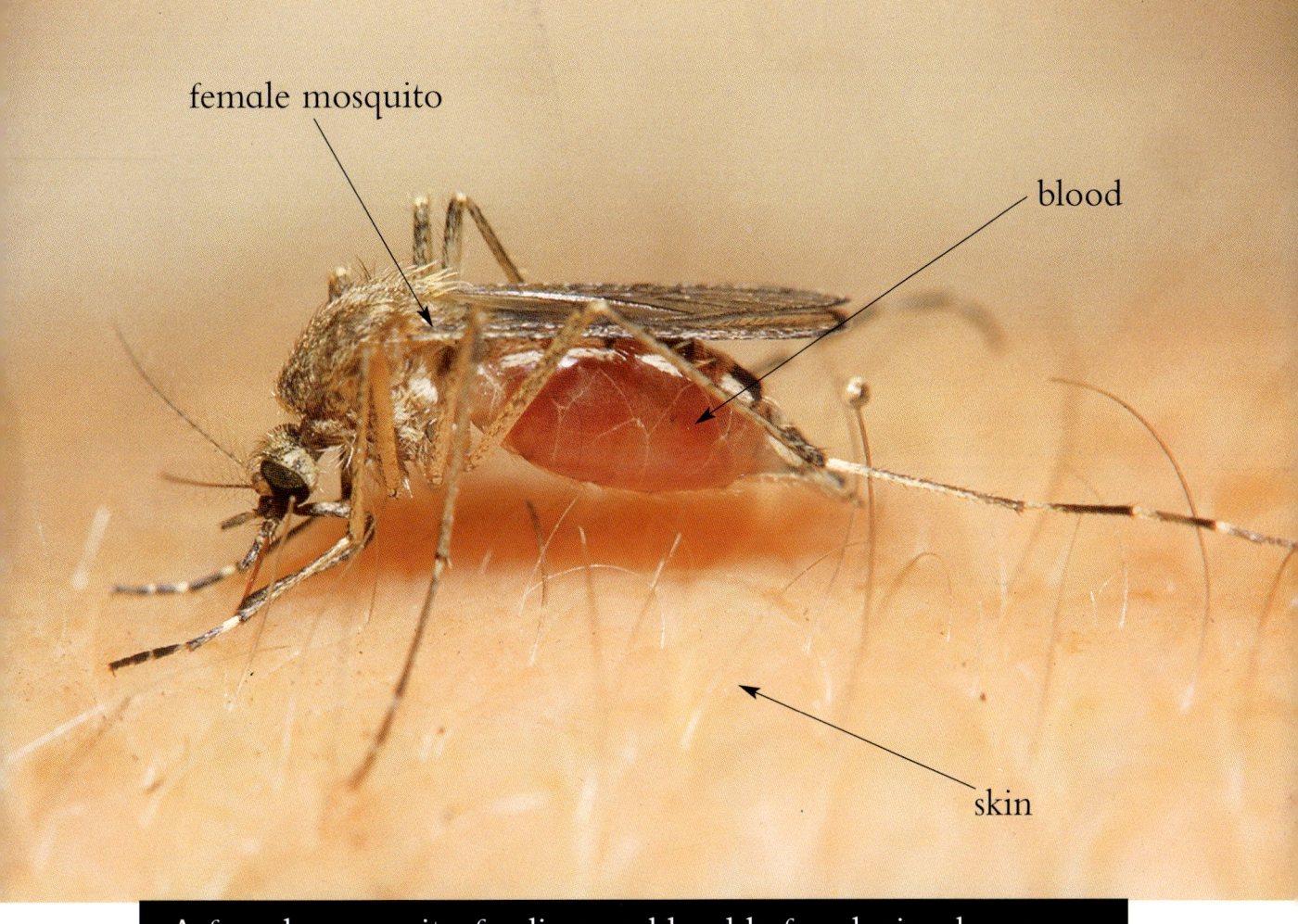

blood

skin

A female mosquito feeding on blood before laying her eggs.

The **female** mosquito breaks the skin of an animal or person with her sharp mouth. Then she adds a juice to stop blood **clotting** as she feeds. This juice may make the bite itch.

Which animals attack mosquitoes?

A bird eating a mosquito.   mosquito   bird

Many birds eat mosquitoes. They also feed them to their young. In the summer, millions of birds fly to parts of the world where there are many mosquitoes.

Frogs, toads, rats and mice also eat mosquitoes. Spiders catch them in their webs. Fish, water beetles and dragonfly **larvae** eat baby mosquitoes.

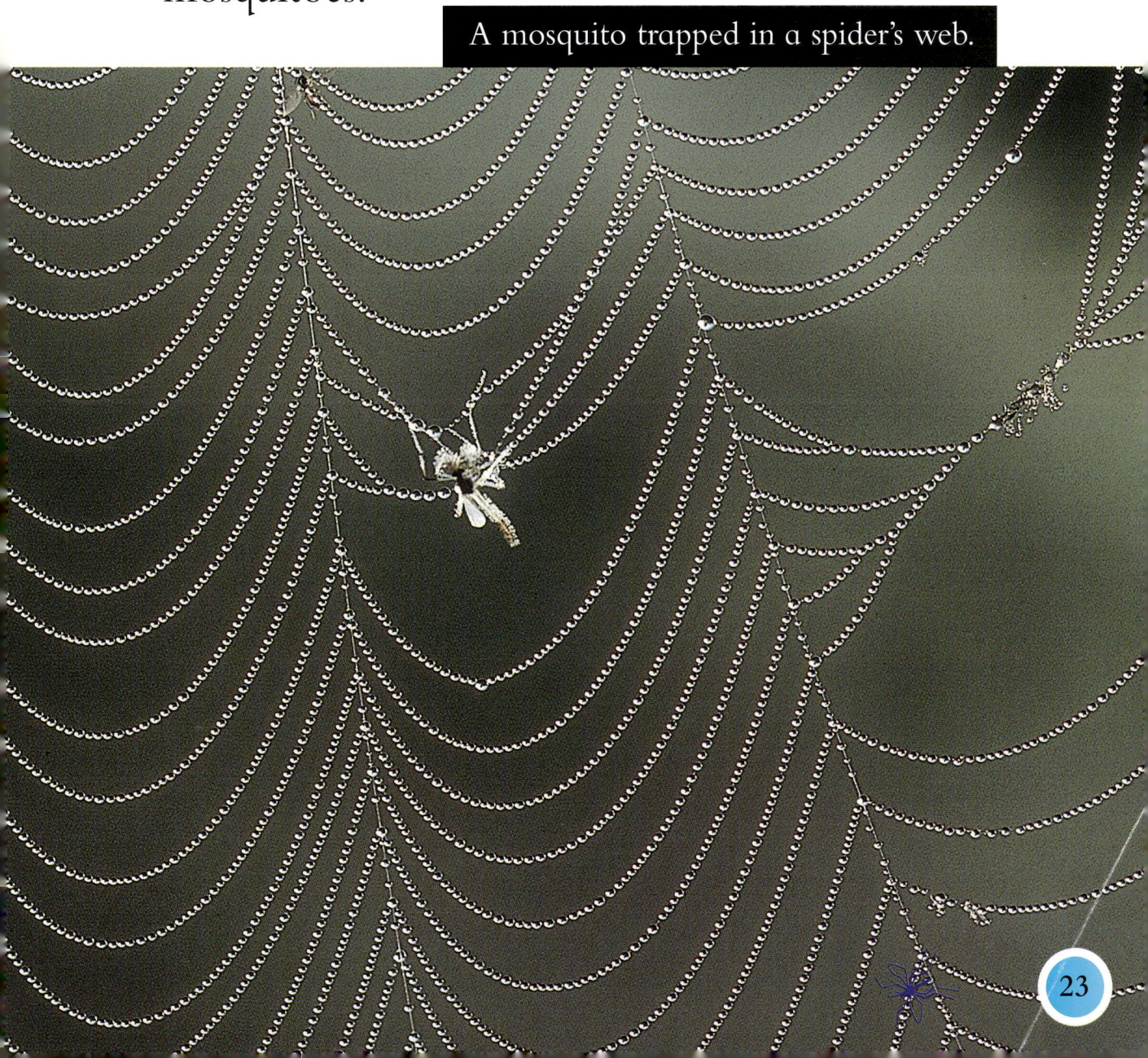

A mosquito trapped in a spider's web.

How are mosquitoes special?

A man with a chemical spray to kill mosquitoes.

chemical spray

Mosquitoes are important food for birds and other animals, but they can also cause harm. In some countries, mosquitoes spread **disease**, so people spray chemicals to kill them.

bed

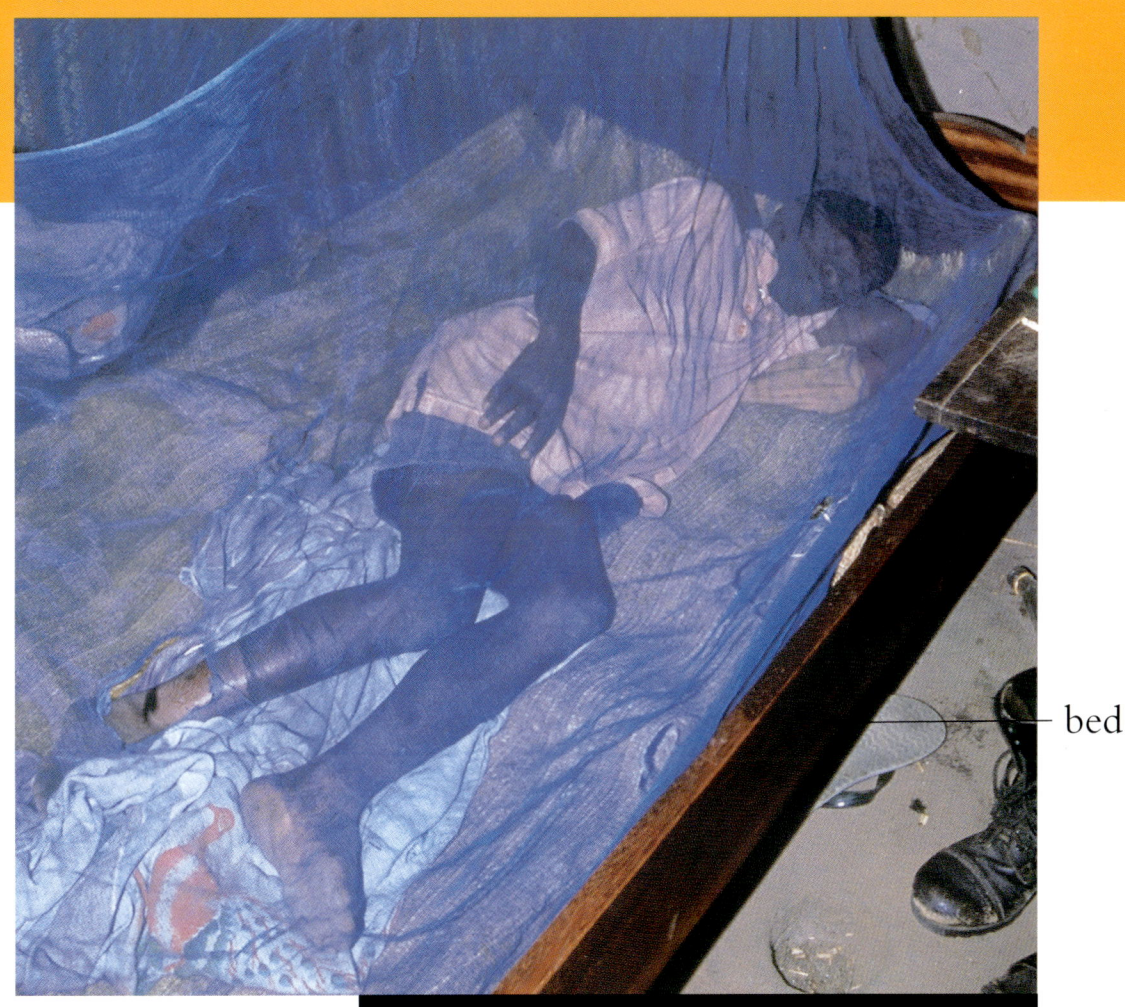

A man sleeping under a mosquito net.

When a **female** mosquito sucks blood, she may carry diseases from one person or animal to another. In some countries, people sleep under special nets so they do not get bitten.

> In **tropical** countries, mosquitoes can spread diseases like yellow fever and malaria.

How do mosquitoes move?

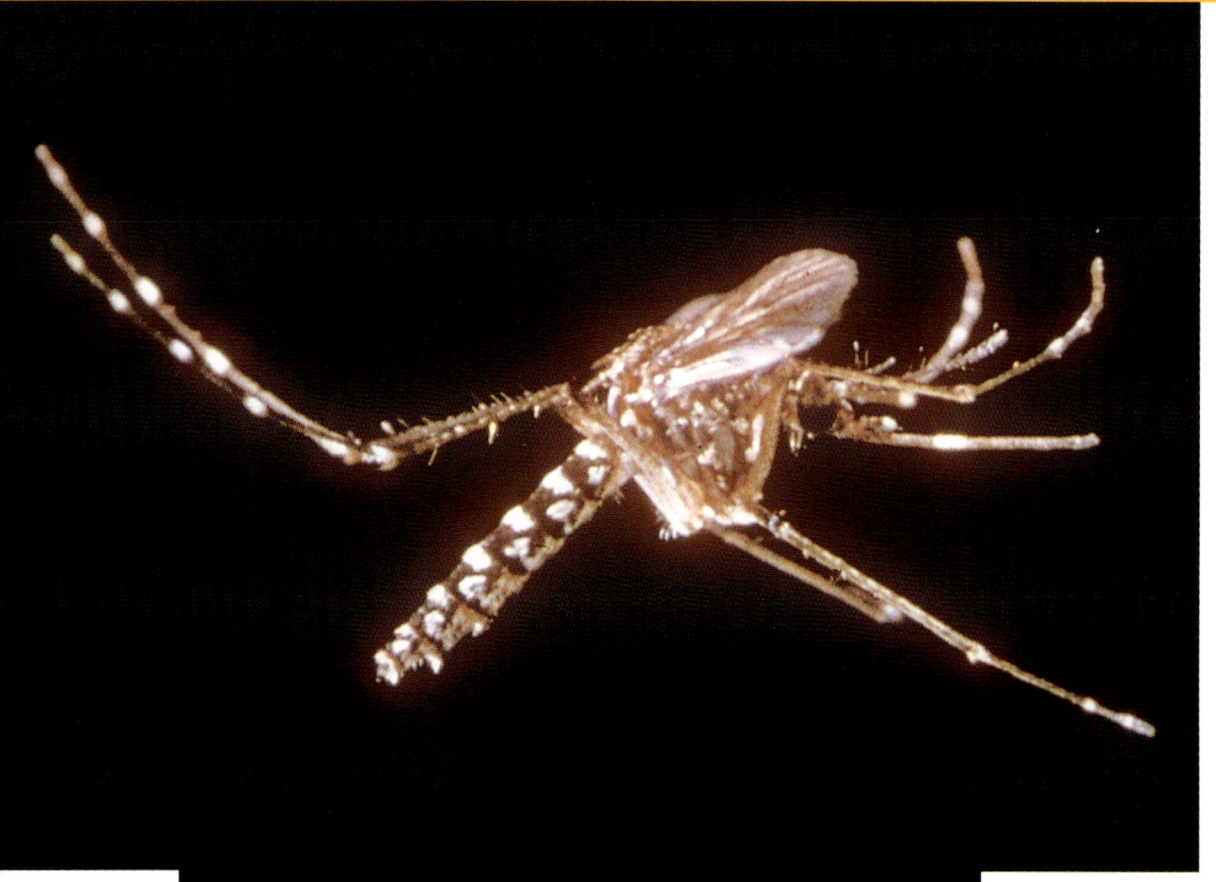

Mosquitoes fly a long way in search of food.

Adult mosquitoes fly. A mosquito can fly as far as 3 kilometres in search of food.

A mosquito can flap its wings up to 600 times a second!

wings

A flying mosquito.

The moving wings make a whining noise. **Males** and **females** move their wings at different speeds. They make different whining noises.

Thinking about mosquitoes

water — twig — container

People find rafts of mosquito eggs in a container of water.

Are there any large puddles or containers of water near your home? Look for tiny **rafts** of mosquito eggs in them.

If you touch the water with a twig, you might see baby mosquito **larvae** wriggle away.

Mosquito larvae wriggling in the water.

Bug map

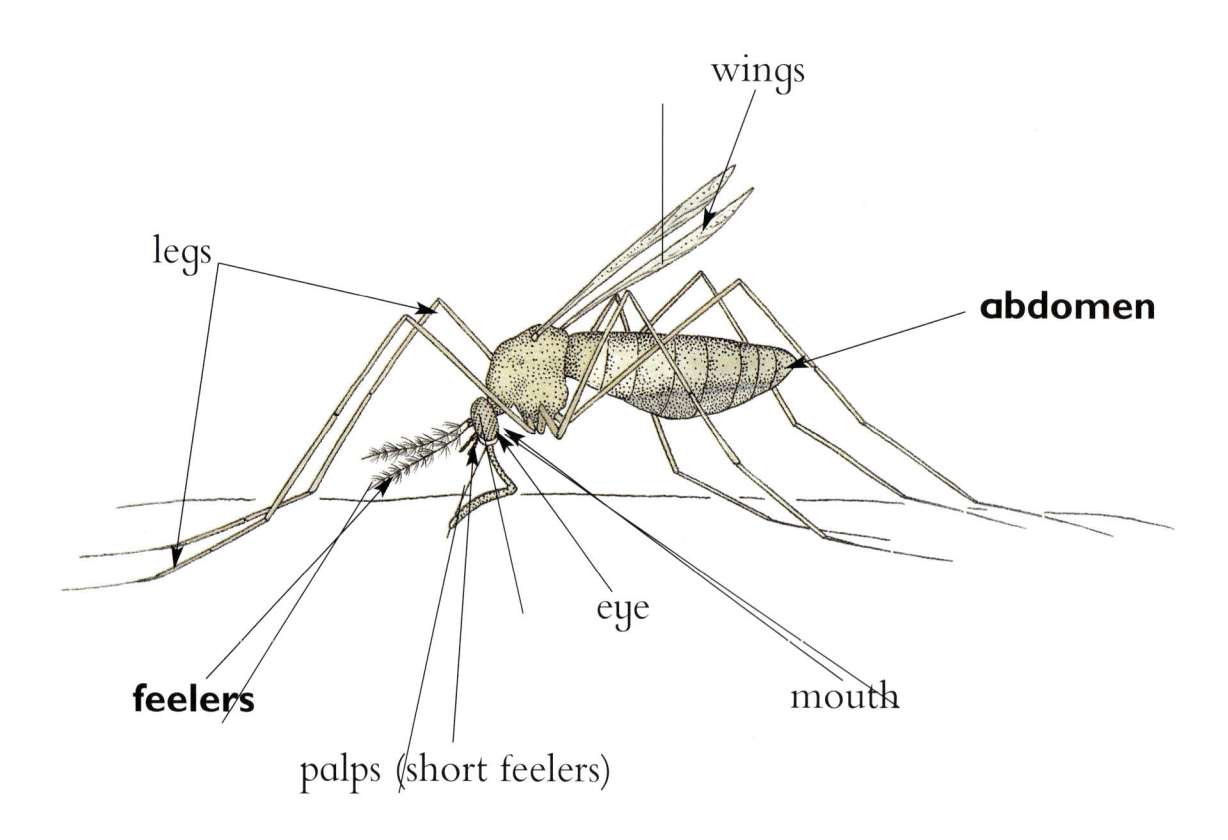

wings

legs

abdomen

feelers

palps (short feelers)

eye

mouth

30

Glossary

abdomen	tail-end of an insect
clot	when blood becomes thick, then hard, to stop more bleeding
disease	illness or sickness
feelers	two long bendy rods that stick out from the head of an insect. They may be used to feel, smell or hear.
female	girl or mother animal
hatch	come out of the egg
hollow	dead and empty inside
insect	small animal with six legs
larva	the little grub that hatches from an insect egg (more than one = larvae)
male	boy or father animal
mate	when a male and female come together to make babies
nectar	sweet juice inside flowers
pupa	case that a larva makes around itself before it turns into an adult mosquito (more than one = pupae)
raft	something that is flat and can float on water
swarm	fly very close together in large numbers
trail	hang behind
tropical	parts of the world that are hot and wet

Index

baby mosquitoes   5, 6, 15, 16, 17, 18, 29

bites   20, 21, 25

breathing   16, 18

diseases   24

egg raft   14, 28, 31

eggs   13, 14, 15, 28

enemies   22, 23

eyes   5, 30

feeding   17, 20, 21, 26

feelers   5, 8, 11, 30, 31

flying   9, 19, 26, 27

growing up   15, 16, 18, 19

hatching   15

hearing   5, 11

insects   4, 8, 31

larvae   15, 16, 17, 18, 29, 31

mating   11, 31

mosquito nets   25

pupa   18, 19, 31

size   8

wings   4, 9, 11, 26, 27, 30

Titles in the *Bug Books* series include:

Bug Books: COCKROACH

Hardback   0 431 01822 7

Bug Books: FLY

Hardback   0 431 01821 9

Bug Books: HEAD LOUSE

Hardback   0 431 01823 5

Bug Books: MOSQUITO

Hardback   0 431 01820 0

Find out about the other titles in this series on our website www.heinemann.co.uk/library